Lucy Maud Montgomery

The Author of *Anne of Green Gables*

written and illustrated by ALEXANDRA WALLNER

Holiday House / New York

Copyright © 2006 by Alexandra Wallner

All Rights Reserved

Manufactured in China

www.holidayhouse.com

First Edition

1 3 5 7 9 10 8 6 4 2

Library of Congress Cataloging-in-Publication Data

Wallner, Alexandra.

Lucy Maud Montgomery : author of *Anne of Green Gables* / by Alexandra Wallner.— 1st ed.

p. cm.

ISBN-13: 978-0-8234-1549-6 (hardcover)

ISBN-10: 0-8234-1549-X (hardcover)

1. Montgomery, L. M. (Lucy Maud), 1874–1942—Juvenile literature.

2. Novelists, Canadian—20th century—Biography—Juvenile literature.

I. Title.

PR9199.3.M6Z935 2006

813'.52—dc22

[B]

2005052638

For
Annabella Nicole Bateman
A.W.

LUCY MAUD MONTGOMERY was born on November 30, 1874, in Clifton, on Canada's Prince Edward Island.

When Maud was twenty-one months old, her mother died. A few years later, her father moved to Western Canada looking for a better life. He left Maud in the care of her mother's strict parents, who lived in nearby Cavendish.

Growing up with two old grandparents was lonely for Maud. She learned to read when she was very young. Books kept her good company. She read and reread the few books in her grandparents' library. Her best friend, however, was nature. Maud loved the ocean, the island's red earth roads, its trees and shadows, the sun, clouds, seashells, and moonlight. They were like magic to her.

After she learned to write, Maud kept a journal. In it she described the island, her grandparents and neighbors, what they said, what they did, and how they looked. Once a big clipper ship called the *Marco Polo* crashed on the island during a storm. Maud went to see it and took notes on every detail.

Maud loved island legends and ghost stories. She pretended that two people were living behind the glass of her grandmother's china cabinet: a little girl to share secrets with and a lady to tell her sad stories. Maud had a good imagination. She used everything she heard and saw to make up her own stories and poems.

When Maud was fourteen, she went to stay with her father and his new wife in Western Canada. Her stepmother made her do most of the housework. Maud was also studying hard in school. Somehow she still found time to write.

Maud wanted to share what she wrote with other people. She sent her work to newspapers and magazines, hoping it would be published. Finally, when she was sixteen, a Charlottetown newspaper, the *Daily Patriot*, printed her poem "On Cape Leforce." It retold a local legend about a sea captain who turned pirate.

"It was the first sweet bubble on the cup of success. . . . ," she wrote.

Maud lived with her father and stepmother for one year, but she missed Prince Edward Island so much, her father took her back to live with her grandparents.

When she graduated from high school, Maud studied to be a teacher. In 1895 she went to Dalhousie University in Halifax, Nova Scotia, to study English. While attending college, she found time to write, getting up early in the morning before classes began and writing any time she could steal a few minutes. As soon as she had finished a story or poem, she sent it out to magazines and newspapers.

"Nine out of ten manuscripts came back to me. But I sent them out over and over again," she wrote.

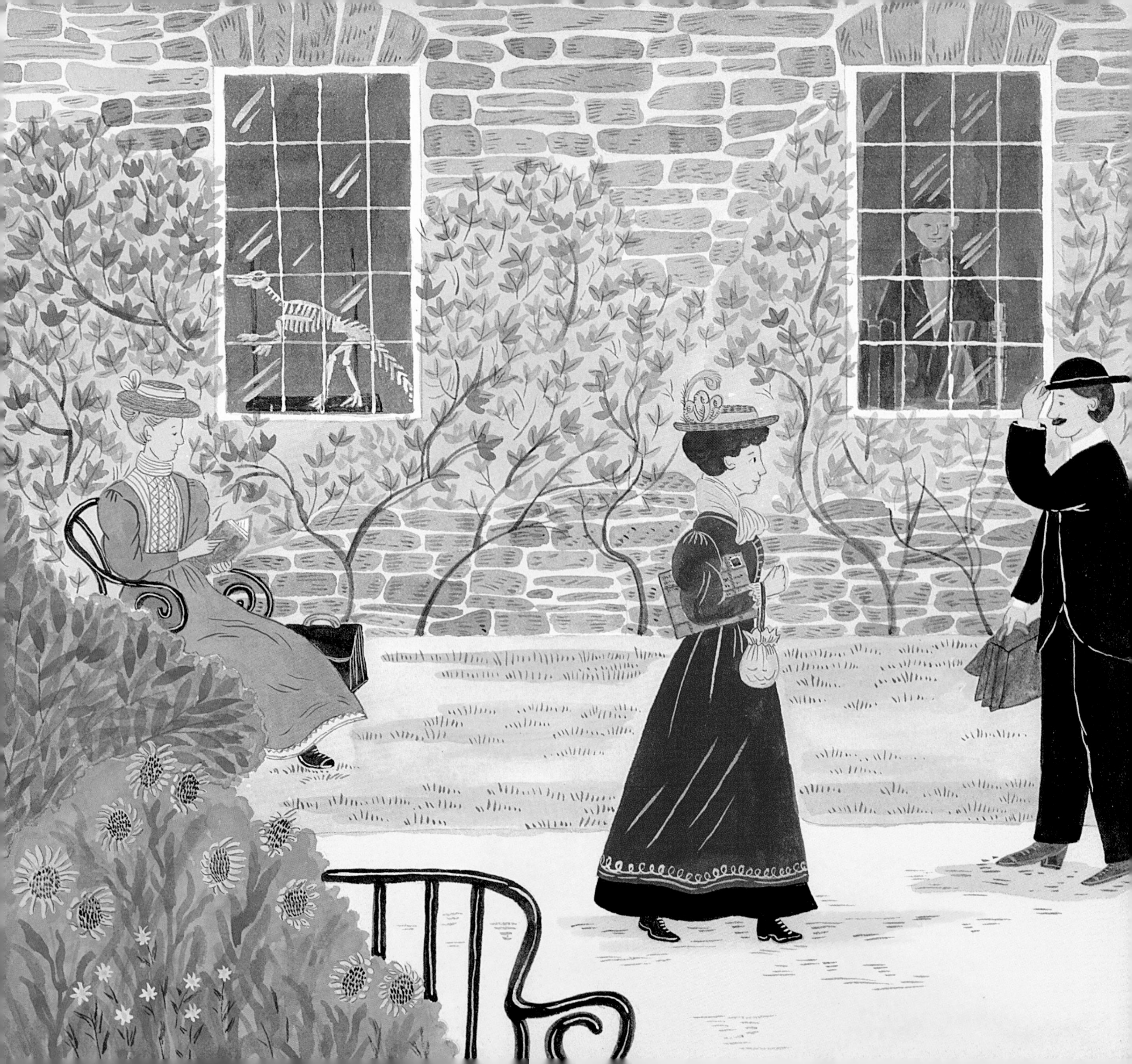

The other students called her "the girl who writes stories and poems for the magazines and gets paid for them."

Maud wrote, ". . . Oh, I love my work! I love spinning stories. . . ." However, she wondered if she would ever be able to do anything worthwhile in the way of writing. But instead of quitting, she kept on trying.

In 1901 Maud went to work in Nova Scotia at the *Daily Echo*, a Halifax newspaper. She enjoyed her job. But she returned to Cavendish after a year to help her grandmother, who had been like a mother to her. Maud worked hard at the housework when she really wanted to be writing.

"I have been sizzling over a hot stove all the afternoon making lemon pies . . . and just getting madder all the time," she wrote. She longed to practice her writing. "I know that I can never be a really great writer—I want to be a good workman. . . ."

In 1905 she got an idea for a story from one of her notebooks. "Elderly couple apply to [orphanage] for a boy. By mistake a girl is sent to them." From this note, Maud got the idea of writing the story of a lonely little girl who is brought up by an elderly brother and sister. She sent it out five times. Each time it was sent back to her. So she tossed the story into an old hatbox and forgot about it.

She became engaged to Reverend Ewan Macdonald, who was a minister in Cavendish. But since she was still helping her grandmother, the couple set no date for a wedding.

A few years later Maud found the story about the orphan while poking around in her closet. She decided, "It didn't seem so very bad."

Maud rewrote it as a book to make it more fun to read and called it *Anne of Green Gables*. Anne Shirley was much like Maud, and the elderly brother and sister who brought her up were like her strict grandparents. Maud took her memories of people she knew and made them into the characters in the book.

"Were it not for those Cavendish years," Maud wrote, "I do not think *Anne of Green Gables* would ever have been written."

Maud sent her manuscript to the L. C. Page Company in Boston in 1907. Page published it a year later. The book was a great success. Fans flocked to the island to meet her. Although she was pleased, her quiet life was gone. She still saved time for writing and wrote *Anne of Avonlea*, which came out a year later.

In 1911 Maud's grandmother died. Now Maud was free to marry the
Reverend Macdonald. They moved to Leaksdale, Ontario, where he had a job.
They had two sons: in 1912, Chester, and in 1915, Ewan.

Maud had many jobs to do as a minister's wife: going to church parties, attending weddings, doing social work. She loved her family and put them first, but writing was still important to her.

In 1916 Maud found another publisher because she felt her first publisher was cheating her. She fought with the L. C. Page Company for her rights. In spite of these legal battles, Maud wrote the story of her career, *The Alpine Path*, which was published in 1917. The book encouraged other people who were working hard to become writers.

In 1919 Maud saw the first movie version of *Anne of Green Gables*, but she was disappointed. The actress who played Anne Shirley was nothing like Anne in the book.

Maud missed Prince Edward Island and she returned often. Once, when she went back to her grandparents' broken-down old house, she sadly wrote, "It was too full of ghosts—lonely, hungry ghosts."

Maud was famous now. She had written many books, including eight about Anne. But she was worried, because Ewan's spirits were low and he needed care. She often had to travel to sign books and read from them to groups of people. She knew it was her duty, although she was unhappy that it took time away from writing.

In 1923 Maud was honored when the Royal Society of Arts in England made her its first Canadian woman member.

In 1926 Maud and her family moved to Norval, Ontario, where Ewan now had a new job. It was hard for Maud to move again, but she loved her new house.

The prime minister of England had read and loved the Anne books and wanted to meet Maud when he visited Canada. It made her happy that adults enjoyed her books too.

Maud fought years of legal battles with her first publisher. She felt that company had not treated her with respect because she was a woman, but she never gave up. She finally won and received her money.

In 1935 Ewan retired. He and Maud moved to Toronto to a house called Journey's End.

A second movie was made of *Anne of Green Gables*. During the filming, the star changed her name to Anne Shirley, like the character she was playing. Maud wrote that it made her feel "a bit like Frankenstein."

Maud died on April 24, 1942, and was buried on Prince Edward Island. She touched many people, especially children, with her books because she understood how lonely children felt. She once had written, "The kind of juvenile story I like best to write—and read . . . is a good, jolly one . . . with no . . . moral hidden away in it like a pill in a spoonful of jam!"

Author's Note

The following is a list of Maud's books. Maud did not write the Anne books in the order of Anne's life. The numbers after the Anne books tell in what order to read them:

1908	*Anne of Green Gables* (1)
1909	*Anne of Avonlea* (2)
1910	*Kilmeny of the Orchard*
1911	*The Story Girl*
1912	*Chronicles of Avonlea*
1913	*The Golden Road*
1915	*Anne of the Island* (3)
1916	*The Watchman and Other Poems*
1917	*Anne's House of Dreams* (5)
	The Alpine Path
1919	*Rainbow Valley* (7)
1920	*Further Chronicles of Avonlea*
	Rilla of Ingleside (8)
1923	*Emily of New Moon*
1925	*Emily Climbs*
1926	*The Blue Castle*
1927	*Emily's Quest*
1929	*Magic for Marigold*
1931	*A Tangled Web*
1933	*Pat of Silver Bush*
1935	*Mistress Pat*
1936	*Anne of Windy Poplars* (4)
1937	*Jane of Lantern Hill*
1939	*Anne of Ingleside* (6)

Published after Maud's death:

1974	*The Road to Yesterday*
1979	*The Doctor's Sweetheart*
1985, 1987, 1992, 1998	*The Selected Journals of L. M. Montgomery,* vols. 1, 2, 3, and 4
1987	*The Poetry of L. M. Montgomery*
1988	*Akin to Anne*
1989	*Along the Shore*
1990	*Among the Shadows*
1991	*After Many Days*
1993	*Against the Odds*
1994	*At the Altar*
1995	*Across the Miles*
	Christmas with Anne

Source Notes

p. 10 "It was the first sweet bubble . . ." from *The Wheel of Things,* p. 33.

p. 12 "Nine out of ten manuscripts . . ." from *The Alpine Path,* p. 63.

p. 14 "the girl who writes stories . . ." from *The Wheel of Things,* p. 40.
"Oh, I love my work! . . ." from *The Wheel of Things,* p. 41.

p. 15 "I have been sizzling over a hot stove . . ." from *The Wheel of Things,* p. 64.
"I know that I can never be a really great writer . . ." from *The Wheel of Things,* p. 52.

p. 16 "Elderly couple apply . . ." from *The Wheel of Things,* p. 70.

p. 18 "It didn't seem so very bad." from *The Wheel of Things,* p. 70.
"Were it not for those Cavendish years . . ." from *The Alpine Path,* p. 52.

p. 25 "It was too full of ghosts . . ." from *The Wheel of Things,* p. 109.

p. 29 "a bit like Frankenstein" from *The Wheel of Things,* p. 171.

p. 30 "The kind of juvenile story . . ." from *The Wheel of Things,* p. 41.

Bibliography

Bruce, Harry. *Maud: The Life of L. M. Montgomery.* New York: Bantam/Seal, 1994.

Gillen, Mollie. *Lucy Maud Montgomery.* The Canadians. Markham, ON: Fitzhenry & Whiteside Limited, 1999.

Gillen, Mollie. *The Wheel of Things: A Biography of L. M. Montgomery, Author of* Anne of Green Gables. Markham, ON: Fitzhenry & Whiteside Limited, 1975.

L. M. Montgomery as Mrs. Ewan Macdonald of the Leaksdale Manse 1911–1926. Leaksdale, ON: The Women's Association of Leaksdale, 1965.

Lucy Maud Montgomery: The Island's Lady of Stories. Springfield, PE: The Women's Institute, 1963.

MacLeod, Elizabeth. *Lucy Maud Montgomery: A Writer's Life.* Toronto: Kids Can Press Ltd., 2001.

Montgomery, L. M. *The Alpine Path: The Story of My Career.* Markham, ON: Fitzhenry & Whiteside Limited, 1917.